The First Lady

Written Accounts From The Pastor's Wife

Anthology Volume I

Compiled by:

Tameaka Reid Sims

1

Published by TRSims Publishing
First Edition Printed July 2016

ISBN-13: **978-1530442867**

ISBN-10: **1530442869**

Tameaka Reid Sims Ministries

www.TameakaReidSims.com
Facebook.com/TameakaReidSimsMinistries

Contributors Listed Alphabetically

Ingrid Broadnax

Kelly Bryant

Yvette Dixon

Jada Hampton

La'Kitsha J. Lee

Eva Joyce Martin

Kathleen M. Reid

Tameaka Reid Sims

Michelle D. Thomas

Kathy Willis

Anonymous ~ Dahlia

Anonymous ~Lilly

FORWARD
By Kathleen M. Reid

This wonderful book initiated by my daughter, Pastor Tameaka Reid Sims is a godsend for pastor's wives. Being a First Lady is a unique and challenging calling for us. So often we don't feel like we can be ourselves because of the church member's expectations. We often find ourselves so intertwined in our husband's ministry that sometimes people forget we have a name, a divine assignment and feelings.

As you curl up in your favorite reading chair with this book you will find yourself in many of these chapters. As you self-reflect, maybe chuckle a little bit about something funny that happened to you and even cry when a similar situation touches you deep within your spirit. Hopefully you will have many WOW moments and confirmation of how God intervenes and guides us through our many seasons of being a pastor's wife.

Enjoy your experience as you read and let's be sure to keep one another as we continue being a blessing to our families and our churches.

CONTENTS

Introduction
Page 8

Tameaka Reid Sims

Chapter 1
Page 11

Beyond The Expectations
Ingrid Broadnax

Chapter 2
Page 21

On The Same Team
Kelly Bryant

Chapter 3
Page 28

The Unapologetic First Lady
Yvette Dixon

Chapter 4
Page 36

Still A Family
Jada Hampton

Chapter 5
Page 43

Embracing Balance
La'Kitsha J. Lee

Chapter 6
Page 51

Finding My Place
Eva Joyce Martin

CONTENTS CONTINUED

Chapter 7
Page 59

Silence
Michelle D. Thomas

Chapter 8
Page 70

He Couldn't Live Without Me
Kathy Willis

Chapter 9
Page 79

Accent Pillow
Anonymous~ Dahlia

Chapter 10
Page 84

Even If It's A Lie
Anonymous~ Lilly

Personal Journal
Page 80

INTRODUCTION
By Tameaka Reid Sims

Walking beside or sometimes even behind the leading man in the pulpit requires a certain grace and demeanor. Pastor's wives are special and have been handpicked by God to gracefully fulfill their life's mission. There are aspects of her life that many will never imagine, and never make headline news. She must be an intercessor, a nurturer, and much stronger than she appears. Because of its weight and responsibility so, many women are not remotely interested in walking even a mile beneath this heavy mantle. To the contrary there are those who don't understand therefore they wish for, daydream and plot for the opportunity to be seen on the arm and in the arms of the pastor. They could not truly realize the true selfless ministry that is required of such a union.

From experience I can say without hesitation that serving in this capacity has the potential to be as rewarding as it is challenging. The wife of the pastor is loved (perhaps even liked), sometimes despised, looked upon as a leader, generally considered a mentor, called upon to be creative, and in most instances expected to be fully present. Seldom do we engage in conversations that address the question of whether or not these expectations are realistic. Nor do we ever discuss adjusting the lenses by which we view the pastor's wife.

For the aforementioned reasons I was inspired to capture the words of those who were born and poised to be First Ladies- the help meet and foundational support of the man who leads God's people. This book is a tribute to the extraordinary God-ordained First Ladies. Rarely is there a non-judgmental platform uniquely designed to unite pastor's wives and shed light on shared experiences. Often times the pastor's wife is so committed to protecting her marriage, her home, her career, and the ministry the entire family has been called to, that her story goes untold or is simply too telling to share. So the words go unwritten, and women who need to read them remain unencouraged. Until now.

It has been my distinct pleasure to gather the thoughts of women daring enough to engage an audience and share what really rests on her heart and mind concerning the calling upon her life as a First Lady. Through these pages you will get to know a bit about a few amazing women who happen to be First Ladies. You will begin to see them as *real women* who lead real lives, have real feelings, and real responses to life as it unfolds.

My prayer is that as you read this chapters you will motivated to share your own story. Therefore you will find journal pages at the end of this book to help you begin your process if you have not already begun. Rest assured someone needs to hear your truth; the good, the bad and the questionable. Revelations 12:11 teaches that we overcome by the blood of the Lamb and the word of our testimony. I will remain in hopeful expectation that Godly courage will arise and enable you to give room to your voice. As you read, I pray that you will grow to hold a deeper appreciation for the role God has uniquely positioned you to serve in. I also pray that you will see the need for sisters to keep one another lifted in prayer and on the playing field who carry the same mantle. Perhaps you will even be motivated reach out and demonstrate your care and concern by sharing a cup of coffee or hosting a workshop or forum to create dialogue for First Ladies in a safe space.

Peace and blessings be unto you, now and always,

Beyond The Expectations
First Lady Ingrid Broadnax

Etched in my mind is a scene I witnessed at the age of 13 at of the church I attended. I grew up in a conservative Episcopal church where the wife of the priest was simply called the wife of the priest. The term "First Lady" was not used in the Episcopal Church. In fact, I had never heard "First Lady" used in a church setting until much later. For the two years that I had known the wife of the priest, Mrs. R., I considered her to be warm and friendly. I remember not understanding why some members of the congregation gossiped and talked negatively about Mrs. R. They criticized what she said and what she did not say, how she looked, how she related to her husband and children and freely expressed why they did not like her.

One Sunday morning, I was in my usual seat about ten rows behind Mrs. R and her children. Her husband had begun his sermon when she stood up and screamed at him. I do not recall what she said but a hush came over the congregation. Mrs. R. picked up a hymnal and hurled it at him. The ambulance arrived very quickly. The attendants struggled to place her on the gurney while strapping her in at the arms and legs and wheeling her out of the sanctuary. The people whispered among themselves, the priest delivered his sermon and Mrs. R. never returned to the church.

I hadn't reflected on this experience until I became a First Lady. I now reflect on it with a heavy heart, and wonder if Mrs. R. had any genuine relationships in the congregation. How did the weight of the impossible expectations affect her? Was she so worn out by how she was treated that she worried more and prayed less?

Living with the Expectations

People's expectations of the pastor's wife are as vast and diverse as the number of congregants. Hence, we must determine how to be ourselves and allow God to accomplish His purposes in our lives in light of these ever present, ever changing expectations. I am blessed to have a supportive husband. When we married in 1990, he had already accepted the call to ministry and was licensed to preach two years prior. I did not realize the effect this would have on my life within the context of the AME church. To offer insight, the AME church has an itinerant system meaning that itinerant ministers are appointed to their churches by the Bishop annually.

For 10 years my husband served as an Associate Minister at our home church. There were several well-meaning members who made it a point to let me know what I should do and not do when I become a First Lady. Some of the advice made me nervous. A few stressed the importance of wearing hats, when the truth of the matter is that I had been wearing hats long before I met my husband. But of course no one noticed because at that time I was not married to a minister.

Mrs. Henrietta Attles, the First Lady of our church, took time to mentor minister's wives. I am grateful for her example and transparency. Mrs. Attles had been a First Lady at more than one church. She was a veteran First Lady. She was smart, poised, beautiful and a voice for underserved children in the community. Once every three months, we met at her home. For two years I attended these fellowships where she poured into us her wisdom, sharing comical moments she experienced. She gave advice on owning a home even if the church provided a parsonage, maintaining a healthy perspective of the itinerancy, preparing for retirement, being real, her favorite recipes and even cooking tips for times we may need to entertain guests.

In 1998 my husband was appointed to his first pastorate, a small family church named Bethel A.M.E. Church in Lynn, MA. The previous pastor of Bethel had been there for 19 years and was never married. Needless to say, this church had no expectations of a pastor's wife and it was beautiful. I fell right into place like we had known each other for years. Even with the absence of expectations, I sought God on how he desired for me to serve. I was graciously given the components of what I call a ministry model that I followed at Bethel and now implement at my current church, it is what works for me.

The itinerancy can be unsettling for the family of the pastor. While my husband was prepared each year for possible reassignment, I was in denial that I would have to leave the place where I grew up, family and friends and the beautiful people of Bethel to go to an area where I knew no one. That day finally came in 2005 when my husband was appointed to our current church, Mt. Pisgah A.M.E. Church in Philadelphia. We landed in a beautiful congregation where love abounds. Leaving a job that I loved and being away from family, friends, streets and communities that I knew the sights and sounds of brought a depth of loneliness that I had never experienced. I cried the first year. My husband tried his best to help me adjust with everything from a birthday party to a GPS. I think it was the GPS that helped me to get over the hump.

At Mt. Pisgah, we are blessed to serve people who are motivated by the love of Christ. They stop at nothing to demonstrate their love and support for their pastor and his family. I am grateful for the group of members who open their hearts to celebrate important milestones in my daughter's life and go out of their way to attend dance recitals, school talent shows and plays. However, like with any congregation, there will be individuals who prefer not to be on the same page as the pastor. There are also members who will decide for whatever reason not to like the pastor's wife. That is to be expected. The composition of this group ebbs and flows and so I pray and I rely on the Holy Spirit for discernment. The pastorate also helped us discover kids do not have filters. When my daughter was younger, I could tell what was spoken in the home about me or my husband based on what the children told her. I had to teach her how to navigate such conversations and pray for the Lord to guard her heart.

I participate with a local AME spouse's organization. The ladies are supportive and pleasant. In the first year of my involvement with the group, one of the women shared with me that while I was well thought of by the spouses I should be aware that there will be times when I will feel like an outsider. Initially I thought that advice to be strange but I have experienced the truth of it. Not because of any intentionality on the part of the members, but it is simply because the group has been intact for so many years. Some grew up together, some attended the same high school, some raised their children together and they have served together in various AME organizations. The depth of loneliness for close friendships in this vineyard where God has planted us raises its ugly head from time to time, however God is faithful. The Word of God declares: "My grace is sufficient for you, for My strength is made perfect in weakness." 1 Cor. 12:9.

It is my prayer that my model will help you. It is comprised of five parts: (1) Love the people, (2) Point the people to Christ, (3) Operate within my spiritual gifts and calling, (4) Display the Fruit of the Spirit, and (5) Be my husband's Aaron. Whether I am interacting with one member or a group of members, I engage elements of the model in my interactions.

Love the People

Jesus commands believers to love God and to love one another (Matthew 22:37-39). We are to love God's people...always. If I feel that I have been slighted, I do not seek out other members in the congregation to talk about the situation and I do not set up camps of supporters. I seek God on how the handle the matter. Understanding that the enemy is a master of chaos with an ultimate goal of destroying the church, I set aside my personal feelings and I choose to love.

Point the People to Christ

When members share with me either their joys or frustrations, I listen. I celebrate their joys, and empathize with their frustrations. But always, I bring Jesus into the conversation. We are either thanking Him for his goodness or talking about what the Lord expects. Either way, Christ is central to the conversation.

Operate within my Spiritual Gifts and Calling

On two occasions I have completed an in-depth spiritual gifts inventory. Very early on in my Christian journey, I sought the Lord about his calling on my life. Together my calling and spiritual gifts are in operation. Like any Christian, the pastor's wife has been blessed with one or more spiritual gifts. If you have not identified your spiritual gifts, make it a priority to do so. God calls his own to ministry and He equips us. Therefore, you should never permit anyone to guilt you into serving in a ministry outside of your calling or assuming stereotypical roles just because you are the pastor's wife. I urge you to seek to know and understand your spiritual gifts and calling and allow the Father to direct you in how to use them in kingdom building.

Display the Fruit of the Spirit

Consider the sacrifices that are made, life in a fish bowl, interrupted family time, keeping hurt feelings to ourselves, malicious gossip, at times feeling like a single parent, and the lack of close friendships in the church. When I have my moments where I am tempted to throw my own pity party, to allow my situations to overwhelm me or even respond selfishly, I look to Galatians 5:22-23 (NKJV), "But the fruit of the Spirit is love, joy, peace, longsuffering, kindness, goodness, faithfulness, gentleness, self-control."

Be My Husband's Aaron

In Exodus 17, Joshua and his troops were in a battle against the Amalekites. Moses promised to stand at the top of a nearby hill and hold up the rod of God. However, Moses' arms grew tired. When he lowered his arms, the enemy prevailed. When he raised his arms, Israel prevailed. Seeing this pattern, Aaron and Hur supported Moses' arms and Joshua won the battle. I support my husband's arms by covering him with prayer. I pray for wisdom, discernment, sermon preparation and delivery, his leadership abilities, guarding of his heart and mind, and favor with God and man. I even lay hands upon him when he is asleep.

When the Lord called his servant-leader, he also called the family. The role of the First Lady is a calling. And because God does the calling, He also prepares the way and provides what we need to operate in our calling. The role of the First Lady has both its joys and trials. It is a joy for me to see our members grow in Christ. It is a blessing for me to build a relationship with a young person. But when trials arise, Romans 5:3-5 anchors me: "We can rejoice, too, when we run into problems and trials, for we know that they help us develop endurance. And endurance develops strength of character, and character strengthens our confident hope of salvation. And this hope will not lead to disappointment. For we know how dearly God loves us, because he has given us the Holy Spirit to fill our hearts with his love."

On The Same Team
First Lady Kelly Bryant

I have loved being connecting to my church for as long as I can remember. It has literally become my home away from home. I was certain I'd be heavily involved in the church as an adult because as a young person my passion and interest ran deep. My mother would tote me along to choir rehearsal and missions meetings; and honestly I was never bothered by it. I enjoyed hearing the ladies laugh and talk among themselves, hearing the music and watching everyone move about with a sense of pride as they carried out their individual responsibilities. A highlight of being at the church during the week would be having Pastor Thurman all to myself! I fondly remember being excited to see his car in the parking lot when we approached the church. I'd run to his office and be so thrilled to share with him how school was going, or to recite a new scripture verse that I was working on. There was something soothing and special about being at church. Throughout the years it just seemed like a natural fit. I'm blessed to say, not much has changed. I know where I rightfully belong.

As I matured, I developed a passion for church administration. I volunteered for years as our church clerk; organizing records, financial reports, church events, baptisms, weddings, funerals... you name it! If it flowed through the church office, it became my business. Our congregation has never been extremely large therefore the need for an expansive staff simply didn't exist. There was a loving comradery that made everything seem to run smoothly and peaceably.

All was well until an announcement was made one Sunday that Pastor Thurman was battling cancer and that we would soon be interviewing candidates to fill the position as pastor. We were all stunned and could not believe what was happening. As the Lord would have it, Pastor Thurman went to be with The Lord. After a long draining process of interviewing candidates, we were blessed to find a man of God that would continue leading when Pastor Thurman was no longer able.

The minute Reverend Joseph Bryant walked into the conference room, I knew he was the man for me! The search committee saw pictures and resumes of prospective ministers but LORD HAVE MERCY, his picture did him no justice. I'm even ticked today as I write these words because the feeling I felt that day has yet to dissipate. We met, and my heart leaped at least a thousand feet in the air! I thank God because after all 15 years of walking by his side, my heart still skips a beat. Our courtship lasted nearly 2 years before we began talking about what marriage could be like between the two of us. With his heart for ministry and my heart for the church I matriculated in, how could this union go wrong?

Initially hearing my husband voice a difference of opinion concerning church affairs took some getting used to. After all, he was an outsider. I expected him to honor my history with the church and to highly esteem my opinions as his wife. I guess you could say he was hit with a double whammy! While we dated I was less demanding and assertive, but soon into our marriage I "probably" crossed the line a time or two privately challenging my husband's decisions and authority. I would have never admitted this about 10 years ago, but I realize now that there were significant entitlement and control issues to overcome. I see in hindsight how I was consumed by the day to day dealings and not nearly as focused on the vision.

Due to the closeness I shared with the former pastor and the responsibility I held within the church office, there was an unusual level of influence afforded to me from the beginning. I felt as though I had an advantage. Most especially during the illness and death of our former pastor, I grew accustomed to leading the congregation on a daily basis and making certain decisions without question. My viewpoint was greatly respected and highly sought after because everyone knew that I was committed to keeping our church family in a healthy frame of mind and moving forward cohesively. I didn't realize in the moment that I was quickly becoming prideful as I fulfilled my responsibilities. Thankfully a sincere and regular prayer life allowed the Holy Spirit to point out areas of concern that were unbecoming in the sight of God before any *serious* damage occurred within my church or new marriage. I cannot express to you enough the importance of REGULARLY SCHEDULED APPOINTMENTS with God. Do not allow anything to stand in the way of your time alone with God. It can save your life, your marriage and your church. I am a witness!

I recall the very first disagreement my husband and I had over a small renovation project. In the heat of the moment I had the nerve to blurt out the words "You couldn't possibly know what is best for this church!" How could I say such a thing? After shouting those incredibly hurtful words I was embarrassed and became so remorseful. I quickly asked for his forgiveness and vowed never to be so insensitive again. The truth is: my husband was indeed sent by God to lead our church. It was obvious. The congregation unanimously voted after much prayer that Joseph was who and what we needed as a pastor. I was in total agreement then, as I am today, but I let selfishness and pride hurl words at the man I love more than anything.

Thankfully I have a God-fearing husband who operates in discernment. He recognized that this was a ploy of the enemy and began to lead us in prayer accordingly. We are not perfect and from time to time we can become insensitive, but we have learned how to fight the enemy effectively, in strategic prayer. We identify where he is attacking and we combat him with and in the word of God. We also have learned to fight FAST! We do not wait when we realize we are headed off course. We act quickly. We apologize quickly, and we go into prayer quickly because we are working together on the same team- moving toward the same goals.

I'm sharing our experiences in order to be an encouragement to you. NEVER allow your pride, past experiences or position as the First Lady to hurt the very one God blessed you to minister with, enjoy life with and grow old with. Remember that ultimately you two are also on the same team! Fighting against one another will never bring about a victory. In the 15 years we have been married there are several things I'd like to share that have allowed us to thoroughly enjoy marriage and ministry.

First and foremost, I am learning to be RESPECTFUL. As the pastor's wife and as a member of the church I must be willing to honor the man and the office he walks in. Respecting Joseph makes it easier to communicate especially when there is a difference of opinion. Respecting time is also very critical. There will always be an ordained time to discuss differences, the present moment may not be the divine moment. Therefore, I demonstrate my desire to respect my husband just as I respect God's timing by seeking God when conflict resolution is required. If I slow down and ask for help, He always guides me concerning the best time and way to talk out a problem or concern. God's way never fails.

The second thing I feel compelled to share with you is something that has worked well for us over the years: KEEP CHURCH MATTERS AT CHURCH! I work tirelessly to make my home a sanctuary for my husband and our family. We do our very best to leave the business of the church out of our home. We have both come to agree that church members aren't losing sleep over our marriage therefore we ought not lose sleep over church members or church issues.

I am grateful to walk along-side my husband and to serve him as his First Lady. I am also equally honored to lead the beautiful members of our congregation as the First Lady of our church. I see my ability to serve them as both as a calling given to me by God and a tremendous responsibility. As we continue to carry the mantle that is on our lives, remember this one thing: if no one ever sees how you sacrifice, how you pray, or how you work behind the scenes God does! Keep serving God by serving others because there is an ultimate reward for all YOU do! Be blessed my dear sisters!

The Unapologetic First Lady
First Lady Yvette Dixon

The life of a pastor's wife can be a very challenging position with all its unrealistic expectations, the hurts, pains and unseen sacrifices she has to make, but through Christ she can do it.

On March 7th, 2008, the trajectory of my life changed forever. My husband at that time was a District Elder in our organization and served as a vital leader at our local church where his dad was senior pastor. This was the day that my husband was installed as assistant pastor. From this moment on, I would now live a life under a very large magnifying glass. I adjusted to a life of do's and don'ts, and continual scrutiny. As of this moment, my life was not my own. I heard screaming inside my head, "My life is over!" Although standing in my perfect long taffeta purple skirt and matching black and purple jacket looking the part, inside I was kicking and screaming, as the tears streamed down my face.

I stood before the same congregation that watched me grow from a little homeless 16-year-old girl into a grown woman assuming a major leadership position. In many of their eyes I had not grown at all. Tears continued to flow down my face, because I knew I stood in judgment, I felt the disdain of the people. Some of the congregation looked on in disbelief, others in pure disgust while others literally walked out of the sanctuary.

We weren't "that couple" everyone expected to acquire such leadership roles. We each had 2 children out of wedlock, our marriage was on the rocks and we were in marital counseling. We did not want nor seek this position, neither did we have a strong desire to lead God's people to that magnitude. We were barely maintaining our current leadership roles which didn't require nearly as much sacrifice as an assistant pastor or senior pastor. I was serving as the head nurse of our nurse's guild, a youth leader and the church secretary. My husband was a District Elder, youth pastor and our church's musician while also serving as needed in various other roles.

In 2010 my husband was now operating as Senior Pastor, without having been installed as such. His dad's health declined and he decided that his baby boy, my husband, should take the reins, and with his blessing he did. There were many predictions of church failure, closure and many people left our congregation but my dear husband continued to stand on the promises of God according to Philippians NKJV 4:13. In June of 2014 my husband was officially installed as Senior Pastor of the church. I did not want this because

I did not think we were ready. I was very nervous and full of anguish because I did not think I possessed the qualities of a First Lady. As you know, being a wife of an Assistant Pastor was one thing but as they say, being a Senior Pastor was a horse of a whole other color. I wasn't a talented singer, I wasn't "deep" enough, and I didn't walk around quoting scriptures. Instead, I was feisty and boisterous, I had a past, I wasn't raised in the church- and I definitely did not have meek and quite spirit. I thought I didn't possess what many people consider suitable characteristics fit for a First Lady. Neither did I feel I "looked" the part. I was not the homely, no make-up, long skirt, big hat wearing type of woman. I desired to be pretty, appealing to my husband, maybe even a bit provocative, so surely I couldn't be a Senior Pastor's wife.

Being a Senior Pastor's wife comes along with a list of unrealistic expectations for example, she should know her place and stay there. I sat on the second row, a seat over from my mother-in-law. I did not speak, teach, or preach as I followed her. A pastor's wife should be meek, quiet and poised, as the Proverbs 31 woman. She should be ready to help, encouraging and of good cheer. She must tolerate the needs of everyone else before her own and completely understand what it means to come second to the ministry. She should dress in modest apparel according to I Tim. 2:9, nothing trendy or flashy. I knew within myself I could never live up to the previous leadership standard of our church and all of the expectations from its congregation. I was once told by a mother of the church. "You know you'll never be able to fill your mother-in-law's shoes." I smiled and tried desperately to mimic her. But those exact words rang in my ears as a constant reminder of what I believed I would never, ever accomplish. Many nights I've cried myself to sleep over fear of rejection and the inability to lead. I was afraid of what others say or think of me. I struggled with self-doubt and loneliness, afraid that I would never live up to all of the unrealistic expectations. I desperately wanted to be a good First Lady and please the people, proving that we/I was able to lead. I wanted to prove that I could be that woman who God had set aside, pulled apart, cleaned up and made whole in his image -a mighty woman of God.

I began to pray, read my word and cry out to the Lord – and he heard my anguish in my prayers and supplications. I began to get stronger in the word and sought other first ladies that I could identify with. I asked for wisdom, knowledge and help on my journey. I even took special classes geared toward the perfecting of the First Lady.

After constant gentle nudging of my dear husband to become more active, say more, do more and speak more I yielded to my fears. He would say "The congregation needs to see you." I had to remind myself of all the prophesies that were spoken over my life. Before He formed me in the belly, He knew me, and before I came out of the womb He sanctified me, and ordained a prophet unto the nations... So I had to speak life to myself– "be not afraid of their faces" (Jer. 1:8).

I began to assist in different areas of ministry. I became the women's board president, ministered in prayer on the altar, taught the word of God in bible study, mentored ladies, and planned ministry events. I wore the hats, bought the suits, went to every prayer meeting, convocation, and attended every service at our local assembly. I even followed my husband to minister at other congregations. I became quite the little busy bee. I did it all, but with the wrong spirit. I did it to prove a point- that we could do this- I could do this.

In Philippians 4:13(NLT) it says "I can do everything through Christ, who gives me strength" not "He gives me strength to prove a point or to become busy." God wants us to serve with gladness. I wasn't glad or happy, to the contrary I became quite frustrated and exhausted. Many of these expectations are people's opinions and traditions, not necessarily the word of God. This was exactly what word warns us of: "making the word of God none effect through your tradition" (Mark 7:13) After being one of the eleven ladies licensed a Minister of the Gospel in January of 2014 I had to learn for myself that I needed to live up to God's written expectations of me and not man's unrealistic list of expectations.

When I realized I was wearing myself out trying to satisfy man, I began to seek God's face, his divine will plan for my life. I was no longer driven to please people but God. Many are the plans in a person's heart but it is the Lord's purpose that prevails. (Prov. 19:21NIV) It was God's plan for my life that I'd become a First Lady, so I had to submit. Every time I doubted myself, the position, or apologized for being in this position, I was calling God a liar. Fear and doubt suggested that He did not know what he was doing when I was elevated- for you see elevation comes from God- not man. It is written that "if you love me, keep my commands" (John 14:15NIV). Those commands are God's expectations of us, we must know our limitations and serve accordingly. Never should we try to please man and try to live up to their unrealistic expectations, instead we are to please God, so we can hear "well done thy good and faithful servant" (Matt. 25:21).

Today, I can say I go boldly before the thorn of grace, seeking wisdom, knowledge, understanding, revelation and favor from God as I continue this walk as a first lady. My walk has improved with His divine assistance and guidance. Through my obedience and acceptance to His will for my life I have a made-up mind to serve the Lord with gladness, reverence and supplication because He is a good, good father. He is a God that sits high but looked low at a little homeless, single parent girl and decided I would be one of His chosen few. For that my heart is full of gratitude toward him.

In conclusion I say to you First Lady- **Be Encouraged**. Love God, Love your husband and Love people. Be careful to "PLEASE" God and your husband only!!!!!!!!!!!!!!!! Walk according to God's plan for your life and be unapologetic of your past. Be yourself- just as you are you are fearfully and wonderfully made. Know that He chose you!!!!!!!!!!

Still A Family
The First Lady Lady Jada L. Hampton

"You have such a beautiful family!" "It must wonderful to be in ministry with your husband." "You must be so proud!" I hear those comments and others all the time and I usually give the proper First Lady response. In my mind I always thought "if only you knew."

This assignment wasn't the plan, I grew up in the Baptist church and knew just a little of what this walk entailed, and what I knew was enough to see it was something I wasn't interested in undertaking. I knew my husband for years before we started to date, I suppose part of my reluctance was the fact that it was clear who and what he was called to be by God. When he was interested in me I had already decided we could be friends, but I wasn't interested in being a pastor's wife. I loved my church home, my pastor and his wife. I worked behind the scenes and beyond the radar, where I was most comfortable. While dating, one day Ric told me "You're going to be my wife." I looked at him and responded "Really?" "That's what the Lord is saying." He replied. I just smiled and kept walking, inside I was panicked because of my concern about being a First Lady. I was never really worried about anything else, and head over heels doesn't even began to describe my feelings for the young minister.

We had been married for almost 3 years with a young son when God saw fit to place us at our own church. I had officially become the First Lady. Because I thought I knew what great First Ladies do and what they look like, I suffered for years making comparisons and trying to fit into molds that weren't authentic to who I am. I noticed even my mode of praise and worship had changed. That was frustrating because I'm a worshipper at heart but I couldn't get to that place. There were things that my church wanted- that I didn't want, and I was too afraid to push against the traditions. Remember, I like to keep things quiet and be behind the scenes, it's my comfortable place although God has ordained me to do more.

What changed? The very fact that I'm writing this says something changed, well after 5 years of pastoring we had a beautiful daughter and a 7-year-old son. The church was doing well and my husband was a busy preacher. And then without warning, the ground under our feet fell away when we lost our amazing, generous, loving little boy after an accident. We will never be the same as we were before those few days in 2011. Believe it or not there were those taking bets on whether we would even return to our church and certainly not many were expecting us to stay married after such a tragedy. A child that has lost their parents is called an orphan. A spouse that has lost their mate is a widow or widower. There is no word for a parent that has said goodbye to their child. It's indescribable. I truly I felt like God just didn't love us at all and that we would never know any joy again.

The depression, frustration, PTSD, anger, sleep deprivation, weight gain, feelings of failure, over protectiveness, mommy guilt and about a million other destructive emotions that followed were robbing us of everything we thought we were. We went back to church and tried to fight back the demons that were trying to take us out. Some days, our theme was "Devil You Don't Win Today!" On very bad days like Jay's birthday and Christmas we reminded one another "we're still a family." We decided on that day in the hospital that whatever the Lord does we are and would always be a family, even the worst of "for better or worse" would not divide us. It would all be for nothing if we gave up. Our bubbly, happy, God loving little boy that touched everyone he met would be crushed if we didn't fight for the family he loved so much.

Truthfully our getting through together was the easy part, doing ministry was hard because this had shaken our faith but we had a support system like no other and it was amazing. We had loved ones that would push us out when we didn't want to go, and babysitters for Jordyn when we didn't want to leave her. Help came from the least expected places. I can't tell you how much it all meant to us to know how much we were loved and supported, it meant the world to us. It gets easier after a while, thank God but the hole in your life where your baby used to be, I don't believe will ever be filled again. The life you've known will never be the same and you must force yourself to embrace a new "normal". Even the way you sit at the table for dinner may feel uncomfortable, we switched seats so my daughter wouldn't be sitting alone.

I remember one of the first times I felt like me again, and not the me that had been struggling to find her place. I met a couple of newly heartbroken parents that needed help. Ministering to someone else helped me on so many levels. Emotionally it made me feel like there was still something I could do. I felt like there was some small way that I could help someone else and maybe it could lessen their pain a little. I knew from my own experience it helped to share with another mom that had been in my shoes.

Spiritually I started to feel like God was listening to me again and actually found me useful. I found myself returning to Him because he had never left, I had turned from Him. I started to feel like I didn't care about anyone else's expectations but God's and that was fulfilling in a way that's hard to describe other than it was very freeing. I had been through hell and still managed to want God and realized He wanted me. The rest of it didn't matter. All the comparisons, worries and self-imposed pressure I had put on myself was a total waste of time because God was using me. He created me to minister, to teach, to counsel and to worship nothing short of that will do. I don't regret the time I wasted doing or thinking the wrong way because there were lessons I absolutely had to learn and to share so someone else doesn't have to suffer.

So what have I learned? Family is first always. Your first ministry is to your husband and your children. You must maximize the moments to give your loving care and attention because once your children grow up you can't go back. Another vital lesson I've learned is unwavering belief and support in your husband and his calling is completely necessary. There is a consistent flow of negativity and criticism in a pastorate, you may be the only support he sees from behind the desk when he stands on Sunday morning. So pray for your husband. He may not know he needs it and you may not always feel like it, but it's part of the assignment of being the First Lady. We know what they stand in need of sometimes before they do, we also know in terms of study, emotional stress, and missed family time.

There will always be a negative situation or person in a congregation but as difficult as it may be don't let it overtake you. The voices of your detractors may be loud but very often their true power isn't what it looks or sounds like. Yes, there are some that can't be trusted and discernment is always a must; but genuine Godly love does exist for the Pastor and his family. Be sure to embrace and nurture that wonderful gift.

I have also learned to be my authentic self. There is more than one way to successfully be the First Lady, and we start by being the person God created us to be and lead the way He leads us. Although there is a wealth of knowledge in some of our seasoned First Ladies, the truth is, this job comes without training. Therefore, I encourage you to find one you trust and like, then allow her to share her knowledge with you. They are an invaluable resource and are probably waiting on a nice young pastor's wife to pour into and help. I have been blessed by some great ladies who are devoted prayers warriors, willing to take time out of their schedules to spend with me, give great advice, and provide a listening ear.

Truly I am grateful for this challenge and opportunity, it has pushed me completely out of my comfort zone and I know that God is pleased. I'm still amazed by the way God continues to work through me and by how far he has carried my family and me. Even through the difficult times God has still been good! He has allowed me to be a blessing to someone else, He still speaks even when I'm not listening, and He still uses me when I thought I couldn't be used. Today we are pretty well adjusted and God has restored our joy. We still have our moments, and have even grown our family since. I am excited about the things that He has planned for us and anxious to go to the next level of His assignment for me to complete. Thank you for taking the time to read a little of my story, I am praying that it empowers and encourages you on your journey.

Embracing Balance
First Lady LaKitsha J. Lee

Being a Pastor's wife and First Lady is one of the most intriguing roles, tasks, jobs, responsibilities, positions, callings of my life. Ultimately, I'd like to focus on the calling that God has placed on my life. This calling as a Pastor's wife and First Lady has brought me joy and pain, victories and defeat. But most of all it has brought me closer to God.

I was born and raised a Preacher's Kid, better known as a P.K. In my early years, I had no idea that I would be a Pastor's wife nor did I desire early in life to one. There were any things that I had to endure, pray through, and live through as I grew up. I did not understand it then, but I better understand now and as Romans 8:28 says, 'and we know that all things work together for good to them that love God, to them who are the called according to his purpose'. My foundation impacted me naturally and spiritually giving me insight into the current work I am doing in the Kingdom of God and what's ahead.

At the age of 31, I married a man that changed my life forever, not any man; he's God's man, he is a Pastor. Jeremiah 3:15 says, 'And

I will give you pastors according to mine heart, which shall feed you with knowledge and understanding'. Well, needless to say, I am yet getting fed and gaining knowledge. I can't talk about my husband without talking about my beautiful children. God has blessed me with 4 wonderful children, two of which are by way of our marriage. When I am not serving alongside my husband in ministry at our church in Terrell, TX; I find pleasure in raising my children, and taking care of my man and my home. Going into my sixth year of marriage I am yet working on the art of balancing my life as a wife, a mother, daughter, sister, friend, an entrepreneur, an Evangelist and more.

The Lord spoke to me about balancing my life by whispering, 'There is a difference between being the Pastor's wife and being my husband's wife.' The things that we must pay attention to and deal with as a First Lady are slightly different from the things that we deal with in our role as wives. As a wife, we must pay close attention our husband and family. We must devote ourselves in EVERYWAY to "our man". Yes, he is a Man of God but God has given you His man to serve here on earth. Serving takes giving of yourself to fulfill the needs of another.

While balancing both roles "his wife" and the First Lady, I found that it is essential and very important that couples recognize the importance of balance and proper communication. We have to be cautious enough to recognize when to slow down and *remember* to remember each other outside of the church and public arena. What happens behind closed doors is what affects your open doors! In the beginning of this journey, God was opening doors and even closing doors in my life, I often say that, I feel I received a crash course in being a wife and First Lady. I am so glad that I am ever learning!

Each one of us have a life story. I'd like to share a small portion of mine. The day I got married; I became a Pastor's wife, a step-mother, gained an extended family, and stepped into the role of First Lady all in one day. Not only did I feel like I received a crash course, there was a time when I felt like I was literally headed for a crash. God was clearly disrupting my comfort zone, and brought some chaos in my life in order to build my character. The feeling of being denied, and being last on my husband's list was apparently slowly seeking to destroy me, naturally and spiritually. Pay close attention to the fact that I said, I "the feeling of being denied…". Newly married and in ministry, I just did not understand his thought process around prioritizing his life when it came to his family and the church. I had to grow to understand my husband- the Pastor. You have to conscientiously seek to deny yourself for the sake of the other and God had to work on ME! I am reminded of a scripture in Psalms, "Now as for me, my feet nearly stumbled, as I almost lost my step." (Psalms 73:2). I stumbled time after time in this area, but I thank God that I didn't fall completely down and give up. I often testify and say that "My stumble was enough of an imbalance to get my attention so that when I approached that step again; I was able to brace myself and walk sturdier and not lose myself once more."

So you ask, First Lady how do I get to a place of peace and walk in a path of victory when it comes to being a First Lady? Well, there is no one right answer, however, I can say that for me, it first took a sincere desire to want to embrace call of being a First Lady that God has called me to be. I also had to accept my husband for who he is. That means the good, the bad and the ugly. It also means, I had to accept what God showed me about myself! Women of God, it starts with us!

When we really look at what the bible says about the virtuous woman, we can gain hope in knowing that our labor is not in vain. Oh yes, know that laboring gets hard, it's painful, and there are contractions in laboring in the Kingdom. Just as there are contractions in natural child birth, there are times you have to PUSH past all of the pain. I often say stop, smile and breathe. At times you do and will get overwhelmed, possibly even feel like you have pushed long enough... while seeing no results. Often feeling like I could do so much more with my time. Ladies you must know that God has called you for such a time as this. Proverbs 31:21-23 says, "She is not afraid of the snow for her household: for all her household are clothed with scarlet. She maketh herself coverings of tapestry; her clothing is silk and purple. Her husband is known in the gates, when he sitteth among the elders of the land. It's because of the work of our hands, as virtuous women, that our husbands will be great in God."

You will encounter many things as a First Lady, some of which may only be shared between you and God! There are times when I have been hurt so bad, not necessarily by my husband. We often are targets in various areas of our lives, it's the calling on our life that causes us to suffer. "If we suffer, we shall also reign with him: if we deny him, he also will deny us" (2 Timothy 2:12). Consider (Luke 12:48) "But he that knew not, and did commit things worthy of stripes, shall be beaten with few *stripes*. For unto whomsoever much is given, of him shall be much required: and to whom men have committed much, of him they will ask the more." There are rewards in our role if we just stay prayerful and remain faithful. As Jesus did, after being beaten, abused, scorned, lied on, cheated on and so much more... You will rise again! It is crucial that as First Ladies, and Women of God that we do not abort the God given assignment in this season.

Do you feel lost on this journey? Do you feel like you are last or simply neglect along the way, as I did at one point in the life of a Pastor's wife and First Lady? If so, it is OK and you can trust God in knowing that it will be OK. I'd like to say, trouble does not last always. God is faithful! As I began to seek God in my weariness, God whispered to me, 'If you want your husband back, then you must have his back! Literally, have his back.'

As God continued to speak to me, I just begin to weep. It became clear to me that I had consumed my thoughts with all of what I needed from him and forgot to remember the things that he needed from me. This thought process caused my actions to become selfish. You cannot effectively serve with a selfish mind-set. I had to change the way I saw my man, God's man. I had to change my stinky thinking and get back to serving from a genuine place of love and forgiveness. It was not easy. It took great effort and great faith.

Kristy Howard shares the following in an article- *10 Things Every Young Pastor's Wife Should Know*: " You don't have to be perfect, You will get lonely, You need a mentor, Your husband needs a cheer leader, Your husband's ministry is only as strong as your marriage, Protect your children, You can't influence people unless you understand them (and yourself), Don't be easily offended, Give your expectations to God, and lastly, Sometimes you must lead and sometimes you must follow." If we as First Ladies and Pastor's wives could just glean something from these tips, it will take us a long way. I struggled in many of these areas and again, I am yet learning and growing. But the God news is, I'm still standing. I'd like to end my chapter by saying: Be strong. Be encouraged. Be the First Lady and Pastor's wife that God has called you to be!

Finding My Place
First Lady Eva Joyce Martin

Tradition has it in the church that the 1st Lady should sit in the seat in the very front on the end of the aisle in the second pew. I knew from the start I was In the wrong place because I found myself at the back of the church at our first charge and that is how it all started as I began to "find my place".

I married the man of my dreams at the tender age of nineteen. Always in the church and deeply committed to following Jesus Christ the rest of my life, our lives were simple as a military family. Everything was in place. We loved God and each other and we worked hard at growing up together in a life built around our faith and families.

Always a "church girl", the concept of Sunday equals church was a given. So when my husband answered his call to the ministry, I had no problem with being a part of his ministry until people started telling me what was expected of me. I never considered the focus that was put on the 1st Lady because growing up in church, our pastor's wife was just our Sunday School teacher. It was no big deal! But how things changed as I now found myself in the same position. In short, the me I knew had to be prepared to become a 1st Lady. The first thing on the agenda was how to dress the part. Next, I was told that I needed to wear hats! Where to sit and who to sit with was also an important aspect of this transformation. I received several "1st Lady" books that outlined the ins and outs of the position of 1st Lady. Can I say that I had major difficulty accepting the suggested criteria of transformation which led to me being out of order and out of place. I was bombarded with all kinds of unwanted suggestions, that in fact began to really bother me because I had grown to be my own person, thank you very much!

As if failing Transformation 101 was not enough, in the middle of this situation God decided to call me into the ministry. I struggled with answering my calling because I did not know how to go to my husband and tell him God was drawing me into a preaching ministry. But when God calls, you better answer!! From that point on life got really complicated and finding my place became a major issue in my life.

No job or position for the 1st Lady is easy but it is even more difficult when the Lord has called the 1st Lady to ministry it is then the people began to look at you in a different light and often wonder how is this going to work out. Well, I'm letting you know that in order for it to work out in a marriage it must always be in this order; God is first, husband second, and then you're calling. Your life is not in your hands but it is in the hands of God. Wait and listen to the move of the Holy Spirit so that he can direct your path. Even if you're burning with desire to deliver a message on a given Sunday morning, if it's not for you to do then it's not for you to do. There is a time and a place when God will say you have been prepared for such a time as this. It is then that you can do what God directs you to do. As I have learned, if He has called you, He has a place for you in Kingdom building!

From my first sermon to graduation from seminary I found a voice I never knew I had. I found more courage to be bold for the Lord and I was overwhelmed with the desire to preach and teach the word of God. In the back of my mind was the lingering question of how being a 1st Lady and a preacher was going to work? I had heard horror stories of husband and wife teams that eventually divorced because one or the other could not handle the reality of two preachers in the house. The idea of having individual congregations really didn't sit well with me either. While in seminary, I received advice, prayers, and words of comfort. Sometimes I didn't know whether to laugh or cry!!!

What was I to do with my gifts and talents? What was I to do with the call on my life. How could I be comfortable with in any given church my husband was assigned to without stepping on anyone's toes? Just be me! That is what the Holy Spirit led me to understand. It is only by being an authentic person can you have peace. As far as my gifts and talents were concerned, the Word said God would make room for them!

Ministry can happen anywhere and so I have had a hard time staying in the pulpit because of my passion for music. I know many might have felt that I was totally out of place when I moved from pulpit to choir and back but I knew I was in place because the Holy Spirit was doing the leading. I was finding my place.

Many years ago a very wise woman told me to never go to church meetings because you will find yourself in uncomfortable situations because of church issues. But I had to go because I was now on the ministerial staff. When I experienced my husband being disrespected or not valued by the people he was serving, I would hurt to the core but was able to still love in spite of how offended I felt. That was when faith and obedience to the word really worked. It reminded me how to love anyhow. I'm in place and at peace.

I am more than hats or colors or seats in the church or conference claims or committees. I am more than the helpmeet or the missionary supervisor. I am more than the cochairman of all women's activities in the church. I am more than the person married to the pastor of the church. I am so much more and it is really necessary that I be allowed to find my place in the body of Christ even as I move about from church to church. I had to be allowed to find my place all by myself.

As we wait patiently for the direction of the Holy Spirit that lets us know when and how to move. We must be afforded the opportunity to move into position without pointing of the fingers or whispers from members of the church. In the church community it is our desire that people would realize that the 1st Lady is human too. With the support of the people in the church and with love and understanding from our husbands, there is a place for us other than just being the 1st Lady. We are more than the hugs for the children. We are more than the compassionate person in position for the women who are broken or need someone to talk to. We are more than help in the kitchen or special dish that is requested when dinners are served at church.

The word of God says wait patiently on the Lord and He will renew our strength. He will allow us to mount up on eagle wings and allow us to run and not get weary. He will allow us to go into those places that the world says we can't if we are just allowed to find our place because God knows where we belong. I'm finding my place.

It is a time of waiting on God so that you can hear clearly what God wants you to do and not what you really want to do. The lesson learned from being called under my husband to the ministry is that my life and time are in God's hands. The first part of the lesson is all about being humble before the Lord and that even when outside forces begin to tell you what you should be doing with your gifts, it is the Lord's voice that must be followed. When He says wait you must learn how to wait on the Lord so I have not minded waiting on the Lord and He has given me the opportunity to minister in so many different ways other than in the pulpit. He has allowed me to do what he wants me to do and in doing that I have found peace. I have found joy and I have found this whole tool of total dependence on the move of God. It is not always easy but it's always right for if we do what God says then we can find our place and then we will be in the perfect will of God not my will Lord but thy will be done.

As I settle comfortably into the place ordained for me before I was even formed in my mother's womb, I thank God for His plan for my life. I reflect on a song that was sung by a dear friend at my initial sermon; "My Times" by LaShun Pace . If I were in control of my life, I think that I would have worked things out differently. I probably would not have answered my call but if I did I would have been so full of myself and puffed up that I would have stepped out of God's will and pastored a church after my second ordination. I am almost certain that would have led to much hurt and friction within the marriage vows. I thank God that from the beginning I learned about who was controlling my life and that all things worked together just to make me the best that I could be.

I have learned through trial and error, through success and failure, through heartache, and rejoicing; that there is no better place to be than in the perfect will of God. My times are in His hands and He has led me to where He wants me to be. I have found my place.

Silence
First Lady Michelle Thomas

In the still of the night, silence is thunderous waves heard in the ocean, beating against the steal hard body of a ship. "BOOM...BOOM... BOOM!"

In the still of the night, silence is tears of dew upon a mothers face, ignited from the morning sun.

In the still of the night, silence is a warm embrace and a gentle kiss upon a mothers' cheek, from the transparent brown eyes of a loving daughter.

In the still of the night, silence pays a call amidst a crowded room. You see it in the clenched fist of a father's hand, pounding upon the ground, searching for answers.

In the still of the night, silence is in the eyes of those standing by watching and waiting, waiting and watching.

No single word can express, the way the silence sounds, however,

In the still of the night, the silence sings a song, of a vanished dream.

2/15/16 – Silence. M. Thomas

Being transparent could be a blessing and a curse. I have chosen to live these seventeen years of being a First Lady transparently; and refuse to let tragedy stop me from helping another mother or wife. I pray that you will never have to experience the pain that I have had to endure as a mother and a wife. Yet, if you find yourself in this situation, I pray that my survival story will encourage you to hold on to God's unchanging hand and never give up on God. When asked to contribute to the First Lady Book Project, I was elated yet a bit unsettled. I was elated to have the opportunity to encourage women whose husbands are pastors. However, I found this process unsettling in the fact that I would be sharing in written form, the traumatic events that shaped my life's ministry. Where do I get the strength to share my deepest feelings of being a First Lady without the fear of ridicule? These were difficult disclosures for me to make, but by sharing my experience, I pray that this chapter will help others to overcome life's difficulties and give God glory and praise.

Shush, do you see that Blue Elephant?

A *"Blue Elephant"* lived in our home, *metaphorically speaking*. On several occasions, when the *Blue Elephant* was happy, he would like to go places, hang out with his family and friends, watch the sun rise, listen to music of the birds singing and make his family and friends laugh, with the sound of his trumpet. There were also times when the *Blue Elephant* would come home and be emotionally and mentally disjointed. Although The elephant's family loved him so very much, they had to prepare for a myriad of negative emotions. This saddened his family, because no matter what they tried to do to help, the *Blue* Elephant it seemed as if their love for him was not enough.

The elephant was in mental and physical pain which caused him to self-medicate attempting to ease or alleviate his pain. The *Blue Elephant* at times, consumed various quantities of leafy greens, found only in the remote villages and only in the presence of his purple elephant friends. After consuming these leafy greens, the *Blue Elephant* sometimes appeared to be at peace. Other times he would often argue, or cuss, have violent outbursts and fight those who loved him the most.

One day, the *Blue Elephant* ran away from home. This caused his family such sorrow. The Father and Mother elephant would search for him until the wee hours of the morning. They searched for him everywhere in the jungle and often came back home without him. On rare occasions, the *Blue Elephant* would return and they were happy to keep him safe. On one dreadful night, the *Blue Elephant* was so sad and angry because things were not happening the way he wanted. He could not get over being discouraged all of the time.

He wanted to please his parents and friends. Overall, disappointments were too much for him to cope with. So one night, he said goodbye and chose to leave his family and friends forever... never to return.

The above story although is written using a Blue Elephant as its main character. This is an illustration of my son Gregory, who on Christmas Eve of December 2012, chose to harm himself.

My Journey

I became a wife and mother to two beautiful children, long before I became a First Lady and ordained minister of the gospel of Jesus Christ. When my husband accepted his call into ministry, I was excited for him and our family. I did not think my life would change, I was so wrong.

As First Lady things changed in the sense that you were put under a microscope at all times. You had to be perfect, and your children had to be little angels at all times. You have to ensure that your husband has an extra set of clothing set aside, just in case after he preaches, his clothes were drenched with sweat from the anointing of the Holy Spirit. You dare not have any friends in the church your husband pastors, out of fear of someone is waiting for some juicy gossip. You know the ones, "Girl did you hear the latest, First Lady is pissed off at Pastor." Or "Girl, you know the first family is having problems with their son. See I told you, Pastor's kids are the worst". What I want to say to those persons is, "SHUT THE HECK UP!" "YOU DON'T KNOW WHAT YOU'RE TALKING ABOUT!"

The Silence

So! How do I share with you my pains, my regrets, my journey? How do I continue to lead, minister to my family and others while living through the pain? How do I muster the strength to share with you, through typed script, the pains of being a First Lady and Minister, all the while addressing a subject that is often viewed as taboo? To answer that question, it is extremely difficult. It takes prayer and more prayer. It is my desire to encourage you my sister to live, to sing, to dance and fight through your own emotions. You have to fight daily and ignore the negative mental images in your own mind. That is what I have to do every day.

One cold December day in 2012, my son chose to end his life as we know it and live in a state of perpetual silence. At times, I find myself thinking of what would have guided him to choose the path of silence instead of living. I may never know the answer. And now here I am being catapulted into a ministry of warning people that their life is worth living. I view this tragedy as an opportunity and not a burden. I know we did everything in our power to help our son. Now if I can help you my sisters to not ignore the warning signs ahead of time and have your family member, or even you (YES, I said it!) seek professional help. With all sincerity I would not want anyone to ever feel the pain my family and I have endured, since the death of our son.

Stigma

The stigma behind suicide from the outside world puts you in a place of isolation. No one really knows what to say because they haven't experienced it. Some people say the craziest things like- "Shouldn't you all be over it by now?" "He was a weak person." to my all-time not so favorite "Oh my god, he's going to hell."

Many who have travelled this lonely road don't want to remember the event; let alone want to talk about it because they are trying so hard to live a life without their loved one. They are not trying to forget not the person, just disconnecting from the tragic event that led to their loved one' s demise. We are trying to live our days discovering a "new normal" without that person around... without hearing their voice, eating at the dinner table without with them, without seeing them raise their children, without growing old with them.

Reaction

I know how I wanted to react when my son died. But how does a First Lady react? A First Lady reacts in prayer and meditation in the Lord, she smiles and prepares dinner. She bakes cakes and cookies for those arriving at her home to pay their respects. A First Lady carries on like nothing ever happened, never wanting to embarrass her family, friends and mostly herself. I wonder should a First Lady going through tragedy model their behavior after that of Coretta Scott King or Jackie Kennedy? They were women highly profiled in their communities and around the world. They were leaders in their own right. Yet, the world watched, as they shed not a tear in public. These women were full of grace while they walked behind caskets of their dead husbands while holding onto the hands of their children. These women were in pain from the deaths of their husbands yet they walked, smiled, advocated, and vindicated the unjust loss of their loved ones.

Was I like them? As you all know, people are always watching how we as First Ladies handle life. Therefore, we must at all times and in all places be on our best behavior. **WHAT THE HECK! I am more than a First Lady am his Mother!** When I picked out my son's final clothing, his suit, shirt, undergarments, socks, shoes, to be laid to rest, "I DID NOT THINK ABOUT BEING A FIRST LADY". When I console my grieving husband and daughter and other family members, "I DID NOT THINK ABOUT BEING A FIRST LADY!" In all honesty, THIS FIRST LADY, THIS MOMMA, wanted to cuss, to scream, to pull up a tree from its roots. THIS FIRST LADY- THIS MOMMA wanted to take the heads off of any and all persons and situation that caused my son pain. That is how I wanted to react but chose not to.

HELP

How can I help you get over the guilt and the shame of losing a child to suicide? How do I help you deal with those who question whether or not you could have done something more? How can I guide you in knowing how to stop this dreadful event from ever happening in your life? And the answer I believe is one second, one minute, one hour, one day, and one year at a time.

Here I am, three years after the death of my son and even as I type the words "death of my son," it seems foreign to me. You see, I know that to be absent from the body is to be present with the Lord. However, I find myself always in search of my son. There is a part of my psyche that just does not want to believe that this has occurred in my life. Doubts continue to fill my mind even today. There are so many questions on my mind, for example, Should I have done more? Could I have done more?

How can I help you First Lady when you have lost a child to death? How can I help you hold on to God's unchanging hand when perhaps all you want to do is let God's hand go? You want to let it go because of the pain you feel in your heart. You begin to question your relationship with God. You begin to doubt that you're His child. WHY? You're angry that there will be no more birthdays, no college graduation, no father and son stories for him to share.

In these moments of tragedy, it seems as if God is not answering your prayers. I remembered wondering why God did not save my son from his own hands of destruction? How could God not answer me? I felt so alone. I felt that God abandoned me. I felt that I had done something wrong to cause my son's death. I hadn't ever felt so alone and abandoned by God. Yet what I discovered First Lady, was that I was never alone. God was with me all the time.

I'm A Survivor

Like He is with me, God is with you First Lady, and we are survivors. God is there to help you survive the pain. God is there to help you stand tall, when you set foot in a room and the voices are silent. God is there to help you deal with those left behind, your other child or children. God is there to help you comfort your spouse who is hurting in his own way? God is there to help you get out of bed in the morning. God is there to help you lead women's ministry, sing in the choir, teach Sunday school, shop for milk, bread, cheese for three instead of four. God is there to help you bathe in the morning when all you want to do is lay in bed. Like He is with me, First Lady, God is there to help you encourage another mother, whose children are doing excellent in school. God is there to restrain you from getting drunk or running away from life. God is always there for you and me.

It is only by the grace and mercy of Almighty God First Lady that I am alive today. It is in the assurance that God loves me so very much and that I serve a risen Savior, that I praise and glorify His Holy name. It is only by God's grace that although we go through trails and testing of our faith, He will never leave me. I believe that God did not give me more than I can handle. I often say that I have dreams, but God has the plans for my life as stated in Jeremiah 29:11-13.

I pray that you will be encouraged by my testimony, that you will be encouraged to live and not die, that you will continue to trust God with all of your soul, mind and strength.

Blessings and Peace

He Couldn't Live Without Me
First Lady Kathy Willis

A beautiful Hymn comes to mind. Written in 1882 by an English girl who the Lord deeply impressed with a ringing missionary call while visiting Ohio. After the untimely death of her husband years later, she and her surviving daughter worked the missionary fields of Africa, where then she penned the famous Hymn 'Tis So Sweet To Trust in Jesus.' Ever notice some of our most poignant, groundbreaking revelations come after tragedy, or a downfall? I often ask God why can't I have the illumination of the true essence of You be revealed before I sin or before the great tragedy? I had to ask myself, 'God why did it take so long for me to really see who you are in my life?' Many of us as women, both brown and white have asked this very question.

My desire, my hope for you as you read this chapter is that you find your peace. That you settle with God in a lifelong relationship of *love, trust, commitment* and *faith*. I wish I could give you some great revelation; something so cataclysmic that you run, leaving that broken weight of a shell on the ground behind you! The solution to Life Everlasting is easier than you may think.

I am a First Lady of 18 years. I will be married 30 years this coming October and I'd like to share my journey with you in three stages. Let us use the analogy of driving a car. In the beginning teenage years, you're eager; and YOU DON'T KNOW THAT YOU DON'T KNOW. Your inexperience alone makes you eager to do it! Then after a few bumps and scrapes and tickets you realize that YOU DON'T KNOW. Finally, you invest in a vehicle of your own, care and thoughtfulness are taken into consideration, and after years of operating this way, you finally KNOW THAT YOU KNOW!

I was 12 years into my marriage before I was graced with this calling of becoming the First lady. Yes, the calling on my life was there before I was even born; but the gift was not activated until my husband was ordained. I was so happy and excited for him! I watched him learn and grow. I was there every step of the way; not realizing the need to nurture my own calling. The eagerness was there but I didn't know, THAT I DIDN'T KNOW. I filled in wherever I was needed. I raised my daughter, ran here and there, met everyone's needs happily with energy with little or no thought placed on what I did and why. I was supposed to do what was expected of me, or so I believed. My pastor was happy; my church was happy- so I was happy. We'll cover happiness a little later on in this chapter. Now, let us continue to be excited about our so called

'liberating Christian experience' in this newly found capability of learning to drive this thing!

The scrapes and bumps and rust can go unnoticed at first. Even the overall damage to the body and under the hood of your vehicle isn't that important to you- I mean 'it still runs'. I can still get to places I could never get to before. Doors are opening for me and I don't need to ask for a ride now. I have arrived, on my own! I know I can keep this machine working! 'We have places to be, Right? Years go by and the reckless abandonment begins to show. I became tired, full of anxiety, pressing through and not knowing when to push back. I was angry, withdrawn, rebellious, and spiritually drained. I was still able to show face- showing up but missing.

What was missing? I could not put my finger on it. The mirror reflected a pretty girl, great hair, and nice clothes. The First Lady accolades still came; but I knew deep inside that I was depleting... slowly. I availed myself to the luncheons, Bible School, mentoring programs, self-help seminars and countless conferences. Somewhere here, my happiness would be found again. I knew it was there somewhere. I mean, my husband and daughter we flourishing while I gave the impression that I was.

This came about at a time when HAPPINESS was the word; "Don't worry, be happy!" The yellow smiley faces were everywhere and whether you were in pursuit of it, killing for it, or buying it, you had to have it! No matter the cost or life that may have laid in its wake. As long as you had it! Happiness was the word and everybody had to have it for themselves.

There is a price to pay with this call. Many envy it never knowing the sacrifice it requires, and for every woman it's different. My daughter was born without sight and I was still being envied. I ask, 'Are you sure you people want this?' They think by taking the First Lady's front seat that they will be happy. My daughter now at the age of 27, dealt with her sight like she deals with most things head on, with confidence, and unrelenting fearlessness! Talk about driving! I was scared for her, and she sees fine now, but I was fearful. She was not. The surgeries she had to have were done during my season of unhappiness. I never once focused on me; but on her wellbeing.

Let us explore happiness a tad more in-depth. It is relevant. I know so many young women who are happy, but what are you happy about? Your comfort in living in sin can make you seem happy, if that is all you know. You can feel good, look good, have a guy with a lot of money; marriage doesn't even have to be the requirement; and still display happiness. No doubt you are happy. I believe that you believe. Your life mirrors that which is glorified on television. In all its technicolor grandeur. Hair, lashes, brows, clothes. The need to show up other sisters and be the best. Chalk up the haters and *do you*. We are happy and in control of our own destiny so much now that the baby comes first, the fabulous house, the clothes, then the man, maybe. His commitment to you in the presence of witnesses and to the world is not even a requirement.

I am not here to exalt over anyone's downfall. As quiet as it may seem, your First Ladies have a story to tell as well. Even in our world of Christianity, there are similarities to the secular. We all have a story. I wasn't who I looked like. I am not here to judge. But to help. I was once at the stage of not knowing that I DIDN'T KNOW.

First Ladies are indeed different. Each and every one of our journeys have been different to get us to the place where God has already positioned us to carry out the call of Kingdom building. We have been depicted as the image of polished purity. Unblemished beings as though we were born with a future of unscathed perfection and silent beauty.

Most people would love for us to have no voice, no opinion, always relenting, ever present and hopefully non interfering! What most people do not realize is that God called us to a special appointment whether in the mission field, pulpit or whatever the work. Without the anointed calling few could never endure it.

The constant expectation and bombardment would cause anxiety to most anyone. Let alone a calling such as this. So, if this calling was on our lives before we were even born, before we were formed in our mother's womb, and I am certain that it is. Wouldn't the one who called us, also provide everything we needed to walk it out. We had the womb love while our mothers carried us. There was nothing we had to perform to get it. God in his infinite wisdom provided for us then and he provides for us now.

The busy years, the anxiety the uncertainty and the stress associated with it, is due to one thing and one thing only. Unless you have intimacy and are walking in the will of God for YOUR LIFE, you will no doubt crash and burn. It is simple. All the classes, therapy sessions, revivals seminars, ministries started outside your local ecclesia, feeling your church or any church does not 'get you' so you're coverless... looking for your purpose or your Boaz won't bring you the peace and the Love of knowing you are fulfilling God's will for your LIFE.

The years I've worked ministry, loved my husband, and raised our daughter, were so easy for me, because as a woman I automatically knew how to "meet the need". But something was missing until I yielded to HIM. After years of self-inflicted neglect and looking for happiness in fulfilling what I thought the model Christian woman was to be; I fell on my knees to develop an intimate relationship with the Almighty God. In ALL that I did, in every step, every decision, in constant communication with the Father, I began feel peace and know His peace as I am walking out this call.

Don't worry about others, those that treat your husband better than they treat you, those that show no respect. Do not worry about them. The problem of people claiming they love Jesus and not His Bride has been around since He started his ministry here on earth. It will not stop because you feel the church women love Pastor more than you... its historical. Pray for them! Only the Holy Spirit can change the heart.

Whether you are a First Lady or not, your first duty is to God. You are His top priority and He must be yours. It doesn't get simpler than that. Walking in His will costs you everything you have, but it gives you everything you need. The grace, the special calling on the life of the First Lady shines like a beacon unto God. She can merely enter a room without saying a word and the atmosphere changes. It is a special assignment. Yes, one that cannot be explained unless the call is on your life as well.

Many have suspected even speculated; but the intimate conversations He has with us has opened doors to the faint at heart and the lost. He uses us in a way where His Kingdom cannot help but expand. The First Lady holds the key to the growth of her husband's ministry just by her loving presence. Many may even reject this love, but love was born out of rejection and she knows this and is able to carry on. It is only through her intimacy with her Lord and Savior that this is achieved. The calling for all women is the same but the task is different for each of us so walk in yours. Talk to God and ask 'What is Your will for my life?" He will answer, I promise you.

And as for me? The guess work is no more. I am really driving this vehicle now. It has oil and it stays on FULL with the peace in KNOWING, THAT I KNOW!

Accent Pillow
Anonymous~ Dahlia

I never asked for any of this. I never asked for notoriety, I never asked to be seen never desired to be scrutinized. I never asked for a parking space. I never asked to lead women's ministry- nor have I ever felt the calling to do so. I never asked to sit in the second pew in the center row. I never asked to be anyone's First Lady. I simply fell in love with a man who had a calling I knew not of. I was set up!

I was minding my business in the library of the college campus my husband and I attended. He was strong, athletic, popular and Greek. Who wouldn't want to get to know him? Not only was he interesting to observe, he was also interesting to engage. He introduced himself and we and ended up talking for hours. That night we even missed dinner in the cafeteria. He was worth going hungry for. I don't think I ever laughed so much since. I hung on his every word! We were inseparable for the duration of our time in undergrad, we graduated, and simply could not wait to get married, SO WE DID!

We managed to get married, hired at the same school and outfit our first apartment as husband and wife. Life was wonderful! We would have loving brief encounters in the teacher's lounge, prepare lesson plans together, talk about our goofy students who were FULL of personality, cuddle on our sectional, walk the new addition to our family, play all weekend and worship together on Sunday at a great neighborhood church that met both of our needs. We had all I imagined and more.

One Thursday evening life changed forever. "Babe we need to talk." My husband announced on the way into our kitchen. Something about that seemed urgent, so I looked up and gave him my full attention. "God is calling me into the ministry and I have to say yes." A lump in my throat seemed to appear out of nowhere. What did that mean for us? What did that mean for him? What did that mean for me? I heard so many stories of women who faded into the background as their husbands rose on platforms that were not designed to accommodate wives. I should have been excited about the news of God using my husband's life, but I wasn't. I felt afraid and suddenly insecure. I was not completely sure if this was a normal response.

I listened to him tell me how God was leading him. I saw the passion in his eyes and heard excitement in his voice. I couldn't believe this was happening. He was going to shift from being an amazing Sunday School teacher and youth leader to become a minister? This decision catapulted me in to a role that I never imagined would be mine.

21 years later, my husband now pastors a large prestigious church his father once pastored and I am by his side. He no longer teaches elementary school but I must. It is a lifeline for me. It is the only place I feel free to be human... regular... wear flats and be normal. Admittedly, I fell into the trap of being the trophy wife and if I had it to do all over again so many things would change. I listened to the limited counsel of women who coached me on how to be the First Lady. They told me to be demure, unassuming, and not cause trouble for my husband or the congregation. They told me to be submissive and never ask questions. I was young so I listened. We went from our perfect little apartment to living in a house that costs 7 times my annual salary. My little hatch-back that was very dependable and paid for was no longer good enough for me, and I was told that my clothes were not stylish enough and not reflective of my position. Before long, heels and hats became my second skin. Initially the changes were exciting and fun, until I realized that things were ultimately replacing what I treasured more than anything; my family. My husband was once my life and now things

have begun to define me... and us. I spend more time alone than I want to, and when my husband and I are together it is usually to be seen and a service or event. We don't walk anymore. We rarely talk about anything other than the business of the ministry. None of this is what I signed up for. I became nothing more than a beautiful accent pillow on the sofa... I mean pew.

Coming to this realization made me see that there is something I can do to change my truth. I needed a new chapter to begin to our story. So I started to REALLY PRAY! I mean I REALLY PRAYED! I started to pray differently. I now pray with intentionality, fervor and regularly. I reached out to women who seemed to have strong healthy marriages and shared where I was. I actually survived being vulnerable, and if I can you can too. I took a leap of faith and I have never experienced a breach of trust. I asked them to pray *with* me, not just *for* me. Those praying women came willingly along with me to fight a battle to get my man back! Day in and day out, we prayed and still pray! We went together and petition to the Lord of restoration and it WORKED! And I am beyond grateful.

I made the determination that more than I want to be a good example to our congregation as a First Lady, I want to be my man's First Lady. And through the prayers of women who shared my passion for marriage I am back to being "his" First Lady which makes me love being a congregation's First Lady. As I write these words, tears fall because I thank God that I didn't give up on what God gave me, and as a result I have inherited so much more! I have it all! If you are where I was, I want you to be encouraged that your truth can also change.

The Lord will turn your marriage around if you give it all you have. Do not lose hope. Change can come.

Even If It's A Lie
Anonymous~ Lilly

She sees me. She smiles at me. She is sweet to my children and gives gifts to my parents with they visit. She is overly helpful around the church. She is pretty and always smells lovely. Her hair is always coiffed beautifully. She seems to be well organized. She is professional. Her make-up is always perfect. She doesn't sing. She isn't in leadership per say. She regularly attends service and is usually on time if not early. I would often wonder why she isn't married because she seems as though she would be a good wife to someone. The sight of her nauseates me because she is sleeping with my husband... the "good Reverend." Her presence in my life forces me to pray and consistently repent because I now struggle daily with unforgiveness and perhaps even hatred depending on the day.

I feel foolish most days because I pretend not to know. I'm not ready for life as I know it to change. Change for me in this moment is unfathomable. There are but two people who know know my truth, one of which I trust to publish- in hope that someone reading will garner strength. I know this makes me sound weak, pitiful maybe. I cannot let go of all I know.... Even if it is a lie. I cannot face it head on, not right now. I have a lifestyle and status that I have grown accustomed to. I have children who idolize their father and find an immense sense of comfort and stability in the home we provide. From the outside we look like a perfect family. Our son has the characteristics of his father and our daughter is a miniature version of me. We laugh, hug, use nicknames and kiss a lot in our house. We take vacations and have regular family date nights. I cannot imagine for the life of me what is missing. What is my husband not getting here at home? How could he sacrifice the sanctity of what we have in our home, our perfect home.

I exercise, I keep my hair and nails done. We have a very active love life. I selflessly please and seduce him. I cook wonderful balanced meals. I support my husband in private and in public. I listen to him and comfort him. I try not to nag and appear needy. I contribute to the household financially. I give him room to breathe and enjoy the relationships he shares with his brothers and friends. I try to be a very good wife to him.

One unsuspecting evening I discovered that my husband's weekly Thursday board meetings are not at all church board meetings. He told me the meetings would not be at church but would rotate from week to week, being hosted at various board member's homes. The rationale behind this was to discuss business of the church in a more relaxed environment. He said it would promote productivity. It made sense so I never challenged him, and I never expected him to be at church on these evenings. Last year, a friend of ours saw him dining with another woman, took a picture of them and sent it to me. I felt as though I was about to die! They looked so comfortable and familiar with one another. He smiled at her the way he smiles at me. They looked as though they belonged together. He wore no wedding ring. The news made me physically sick for days leaving me unable to eat, sleep, care for the children or work. While working through my "virus" I coached myself out of the bed and back into my position as wife, mother, professional and First Lady. I am numb most days... I hurt and am unable to mentally or emotionally process where I am.

There are some Sundays I weep uncontrollably while preparing for church. When asked "What's wrong?" I responded by saying the tears were just part of my worship. The children haven't bothered me since. Somehow by the time we pull up in the church I manage to pull it together. I catch myself staring at my husband from the third pew. I look at him and wonder who that man is and how he could possibly be living a double life. There have even been times

I imagine myself making a scene, right there in the middle of service. I want to scream! I want to choke him. I want to throw bibles, boxes of tissue, shoes, and purses- anything I can get my hands on. Instead I sit there, smiling, encouraging, raising my hands and faking my way through yet another worship service. I hate it.

For the time being I usually cope by crying, journaling and praying. I don't seem to have the attention span to read my bible. The words seem to become blurred on the page. I get angry and pray. I get sad and pray. I feel depressed and pray. I become afraid and pray. I don't share my hurt with because I don't have a plan yet and I don't know who to trust.

Everyone loves and respects my husband. He is a talented preacher, well educated, and charismatic. Within minutes of meeting him, many feel as though they have known him forever. His smile, his warmth, his ability to capture any audience makes him easy to like, love and admire. I don't know if God will heal the fracture that has taken place within the walls of our home but for some reason I am hopeful. I don't know why.

I never imagined this would be my story. My ugly truth. I used to look at women who stayed married while in adulterous situations and think ill of them. I would see them as desperate and judge them, and now here I am; praying for the strength to wake up out of this terrible nightmare. I used to have faith, but for the moment I seem to have lost it. This painful reality makes me wonder why has God deserted me. I cry out often "Why!!!!!" and hear nothing in return. It seems as if God is not listening, at least not to me. Deep in my spirit, I know I will make it through, and I know ultimately that God is the only force sustaining me in this moment. It just feels so bad in the moment. My spirit and heart are so very bruised.

I doubt many realize that there are so many First Ladies who feel this way because we smile, and stay in position. We smile and are held together by strings. We smile and are coming apart at the seams. We smile but want to cuss like drunken sailors. We smile but want to run away and hide. We smile and are captured in beautiful photographs with our husbands and children..... even if it's a lie.

Journal Your Personal Story

Begin recording your personal journey as a First Lady!

_____

_____

_____

_____

_____

_____

_____

_____

_____

_____

_____

_____

_____

_____

Other Resources Available Through Tameaka Reid Sims
Ministries at www.TameakaReidSims.com
Digital Versions at www.Amazon.com

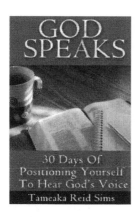

This 30 Day Interactive
Devotional Experience
will change your relationship
with God by engaging the
reader with a scripture,
prayer and
daily assignments.
$15.00

An ideal resource for leaders
of Women's ministry:
Season & Event Themes
Ice Breakers
Ways to Make Prayer Fun
Engaging Group Ideas
Outing Ideas
$20.00

Made in the USA
Charleston, SC
26 August 2016